The PREACHER and the PROSTITUTE

E. K. Bailey

MOODY PUBLISHERS
CHICAGO

Text design and illustrations by Coffee Bean Design

Cover design by Smartt Guys

Library of Congress Cataloging-in-Publication Data

Bailey, E.K., 1945-
The preacher and the prostitute / E.K. Bailey.
p. cm.
ISBN: 0-8024-3731-1
1. Hosea (Biblical prophet) 2. Bible stories, English–O.T. Hosea. 3. Conversion—Christianity. I. Title.

BS580.H6B35 2004
224'.609505–dc22

2004012335

1 3 5 7 9 10 8 6 4 2

Printed in the United States of America

In memory of Dr. E. K. Bailey,
whose life and love was to preach
the incomparable gospel of Jesus Christ,
declaring God's Truth with compassion
and without compromise.

He stayed faithful to God's call even to the end,
and now he awaits with His Lord
the wedding feast of the Lamb.

The PREACHER and the PROSTITUTE

SHALOM. MY NAME IS HOSEA. I served Jehovah as one of His prophets. My professional ministry, recorded in the Bible, took place primarily in the northern kingdom of Israel between 750

and 725 B.C. I was given one of the most unusual assignments ever given to one in my profession.

Some of your contemporaries, who are a part of the apostolic tradition, thought my story possesses worldwide significance. Therefore, I was summoned here and instructed to share with you brief excerpts from my biography.

The most interesting segment of my life began as I was meandering along the countryside. I had just concluded one of my many prophetic crusades and was descending the heights of Mount Tabor.

SUDDENLY I WAS APPREHENDED BY A STRANGE AND INVISIBLE PRESENCE. THIS PRESENCE WAS SO MYSTERIOUS THAT I WAS AT ONCE BOTH TERRIFIED AND FASCINATED.

Although rare, this experience was not new to me. Having been there before, I was aware that I was in the presence of the One who is eternal.

When He spoke to me, His voice seemed to have been riding the bosom of the wind. Slowly it enveloped me, causing me to feel as if I was standing at the center of a whirlwind.

"Hosea, I must speak to you concerning the infidelity of My people," God said. "You do remember our covenantal agreement, that Israel will be My people and that I would be her God? But now, Hosea, because of her apostasy, her idolatry, and her immorality, her goodness has become like the morning dew. It has faded away.

"THROUGH HER CONDUCT SHE HAS FRACTURED OUR FRIENDSHIP—RUPTURED OUR RELATIONSHIP. SHE HAS ALLOWED STRANGE GODS TO ENCROACH UPON MY PRIVATE DOMAIN."

As God was speaking, I did not say much; in fact, I did not speak at all. What does one say when God is speaking? Gradually, I slumbered into an altered state of consciousness.

While I hung in a state of semiconsciousness, God took me on a historical journey where He allowed me to see Israel's history. I watched His chosen people vacillate over and over in their commitment to Yahweh, and in situation after situation I saw Israel go whoring after other gods.

As I listened to God review that painful past, HIS VOICE WAS LIKE THAT OF A MAN WHO HAD KNOWN EXCRUCIATING PAIN . . . pain only known to those who have had their love rejected.

As I listened to the tone of the conversation, I just knew that God was about to say to me that He was going to destroy Israel. I wanted to hear Him say, "I am planning to annihilate Israel so that not even her memory will be part of the annals of human history." Yet to my utter amazement, instead He said, "Hosea, I will save Israel, not by bow, nor by sword, nor by battle, nor by horsemen, but I will save her by the power of My love."

Recovering from my near-catatonic state, slowly I was able to focus again on what was happening. I said, "Lord I am sure that all of Israel will be delirious with delight to hear of Your merciful reprieve. However, I am puzzled about my role in Your relationship with this rebellious people."

Then He responded,
"Hosea, I want you to get married.

"You see, I need a living and visible model. I want you to be My visible allegory, My living dramatization, so that My people will understand the nature and essence of My message.

"However, Hosea," God continued, "although I have chosen you as the conduit through which My message will travel, I need to inform you that additional preparation is needed before you are sufficiently ready to represent Me.

"To let you know that this assessment has not come about without careful observation and evaluation, I listened in during your last crusade, and what I heard was troubling to My Spirit. On the positive side you were eloquent in speech, you were knowledgeable of your subject, you were excellent in your delivery and astute in the use of Scripture; yet there was an absence of balance. You epitomized a lop-sided, errant theology that made it clear to Me that you have not fully comprehended My cosmopolitan concepts of salvation. You are yet too narrow and parochial in your understanding of how My love is far-reaching and all-embracing.

"Your theology is hemmed in by habit; your sociology is crimped by customs; your anthropology is trapped by tradition; your psychology is jailed by your Jewishness. Therefore, I have decided that the best way to equip you to accurately reflect the true essence of My heart is to send you through the crucible of domestic difficulty."

Aha, marriage! I said to myself. *That's not so bad, especially when you have an omnipotent God personally selecting the bride.*

Then it occurred to me that God's timing is absolutely wonderful. It had been only a few days prior that I had had a conversation with myself. I had said,

Prophet, it is time that you take for yourself a wife.

And it just so happens that I have had my eye on this certain young lady. Although I have not spoken to her father about my intentions, I believed from my observations that she would make an outstanding prophet's wife. She is not only beautiful, but she comes out of a strong Orthodox Jewish background. She has an impeccable reputation, she seems to have a heart for God, and she comes to all of my crusades. She helps me to pass out Ten Commandment tracts. I believe that she would be a compatible life partner.

With deep compassion, God said, "Hosea, I know fully well the girl about whom you are thinking. You are a good judge of character, and you are right, she will make someone an

excellent wife. Nevertheless, Hosea, she is not the one that I have in mind for you.

"The girl whom I have chosen for you does not come from an Orthodox Jewish background. She has never been to any of your crusades. She has seldom heard My name. Worst of all, she is a pagan prostitute. Today some might even call her a 'hoochie.' This is the girl whom I have sovereignly selected to be your life partner."

Gradually I sank into an emotional abyss, and my life passed before my eyes. For days, I sank farther and farther into the darkness of depression. Do I have to tell any of you how I felt? I think not. Do I have to describe to you the internal conflicting impulses that were warring beneath my skin? On one side was the unbridled loyalty to Yahweh, and on the other was my reverence for my Jewish heritage, which would quickly condemn such an irreparable act.

"Come on, lay your icy fingers upon me, and freeze my blood in his veins. Come on, death, and use the blade of your dreaded chisel! Dismantle the properties of my defenseless body."

I stood there so long that it seemed time had stood still. Fearfully I opened one eye to see if I could catch a glimpse of death on the back of its pale horse, charging toward my destruction. Then I opened my other eye and noticed that death was nowhere in sight. Quickly I sought to put as much distance between myself and that place of gloom. But as I put my ambulatory system in gear to ease away from that moment in time, God spoke.

"The girl's name is Gomer, and she is the one I have chosen for you to marry."

Still angry, I said, "God, who wants to be married to a woman with a name like Gomer?" Today you look for women with names like Shenikwa and Kiesha, or Jennifer and Elizabeth, not Gomer. In my day we liked Ruth, Deborah, and Miriam. But Gomer?

Pressing my objection even further, I said to God, "OK, maybe I will consider marriage, but can You give some plausible reasons to marry a wayward woman? How will I explain it to the prophetic fraternity? What about my family and friends? I will never be able to face the people of Israel as a prophet again. None of these groups will believe that God told me to do such a ridiculous things."

My last effort at trying to dissuade God from accomplishing His purpose, I believe, was my most cunning attempt and cleverest use of human logic.

In my attempt at throwing back at God a little reverse psychology, I said, "God, I recall You saying that whatever we do should be done to the glory of God."

This is where I thought I had Him. I said,

"WHAT GLORY WOULD YOU GET FROM A PROPHET MARRYING A PROSTITUTE?

What glory would You get when there is a union between piety and promiscuity? What glory would You get when there is a confluence of the devilish and the divine? What glory would You get from the joining of the sacred and the secular? What glory would You get from an intercourse of the celestial and the terrestrial? What glory would You get from an allegiance between the horizontal and the perpendicular, from a coupling of the heavenly and the hellish? These things are by nature diametrically opposed to one another."

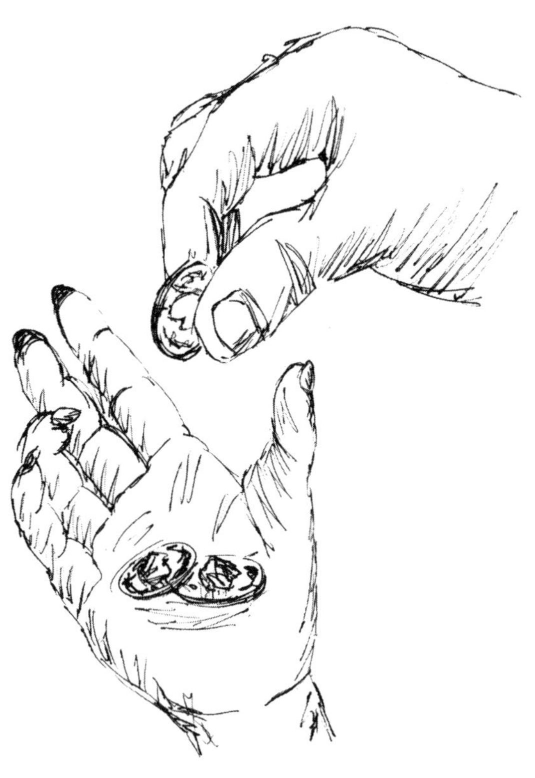

Just as I tried to prove myself by exhibiting human erudition, the overshadowing wisdom of God stepped in to teach me a humbling and invaluable lesson. God said, "Hosea, do you remember the day I called you to be a prophet?"

"Of course; how can I ever forget it?" I answered. "My life was changed forever."

"You will remember that I told you I was calling you into a divine human partnership," the Lord continued. "I told you that in this partnership, I am the senior partner, and as the senior partner, I reserve the right to make sovereign decisions without your approval.

"In keeping with that understanding, at this point I refuse to give any reason for My request. Even if I give My reasons, you are too myopic to see their value. Therefore, I will not subject My divine wisdom to your shortsightedness or scrutiny. Further, I do not need your approval.

"The way this works is, I have made My request . . . now I am waiting on your response. I will not show some supernatural phenomenon to convince you to commit to Me. Your commitment is based on your faith—not faith in what I do but faith in who I am. Hosea, it is by faith that you follow Me, faith not based on how practical I am or how much sense I make but faith based on how much trust you have in the God who I am. Faith teaches you to follow God's heart when you cannot trace God's hand!"

I found myself walking in the path of obedience. The farther I walked, the brighter things became. The physical path did not get brighter, but my spiritual understanding did. Have you found it to be that way? As you stop wrestling with God and start obeying Him, He sheds His illuminating light on the darkness of your understanding.

As I walked in the illuminating light of obedience, God quickly began to unravel the seemingly nonsensical nature of this paradoxical command. God told me that this improbable partnership that wedded the prophet and the prostitute was a dramatization of the extraordinary reality that God loves the unlovely.

God chose Gomer so that He could point to one of the most debased and despicable of all human activities to show us that His unfailing love is never ending and the reach of His love has no limits. God would use the life of an unfaithful wife to demonstrate the reality that you can break God's heart but you can never break His love.

Yes, I believe God desires that the male and the female Gomers of history know the relentlessness of divine love, and that such love will follow you into the stench of a hog pen until it rescues the unfaithful and transforms their desperate lives. The good news of the Gospel that your New Testament declares is that no Gomer, regardless how godless her (or his) sin, can fall so deep and hard that they fall outside the realm and reach of God's love.

For fear that some of you have missed the significance of God's love for the unlovely, let me remind you that all of us are apart of the unlovely crowd. Your Bible states,

"ALL OF US LIKE SHEEP HAVE GONE ASTRAY." IT ALSO SAYS, "ALL HAVE SINNED AND FALL SHORT OF THE GLORY OF GOD"

(ISAIAH 53:6; ROMANS 3:23).

What these statements mean is that my wife, Sister Gomer, is related not only to me but also to all of us. She is kinfolk. The blood that runs through Gomer's veins is the blood of Adam. The blood of Adam is the same blood of all men and women.

Perhaps your sin is not Gomer's sin, but all sin is reprehensible in the sight of God. Therefore, your sin places you into the unlovely crowd.

If salvation was based on works or according to how hard a person tries, then Gomer would have scored high on the "works chart." Even now, it moves me to tears when I think about how hard my wife tried. The girl tried . . . she really did try.

I recall the day she returned home after a delightful shopping spree. The scintillating smile she wore on her face could not begin to portray the depth of joy that welled up in her heart. She brought home from the mall a colorful but tasteful wardrobe that would complement her husband in his highly visible role as one of Yahweh's most popular prophets. She was so pleased with her new look that she threw out all of her old clothes. She said, "I am a prophet's wife now."

She not only changed her wardrobe, but she also changed the color of her hair and lipstick—she changed everything! She was trying.

She even changed the time she went down to the village well to draw water. She even knew how critical it was to change the ungodly crowd that she was once associated with.

She tried. . . . Oh, she tried.

However, like a beast of prey she was caught between two ferocious attackers. On one side she faced the awful internal pull of the wiles of her old world. On the other, she experimented with the terrible external push by the self-proclaimed pious. This pull and push provoked within a war of wills wherein the commitment to God was at stake. She struggled with her unconverted passions, which were constantly being prodded by the lips and arms of her many lovers. But she also wrestled with the push of those self-righteous temple goers who always sought to make themselves better at the expense of others. In attempting to hide their guilt, those self-seeking pious individuals constantly pointed their accusatory fingers at the lives of others.

Every time my wife walked down the road, some of the temple folks would say, "There goes that old . . . !" You know those terrible ungodly names that people use. They pushed her and pushed her, until she finally broke.

One day she burst into the house. With tears steaming down, she cried out to me,

"Hosea, is this what your religion is all about? I don't want any part of it!"

I knew then that it was only a matter to time before she slid back in the wickedness of her past. It started very subtly and slowly. It was little by little, bit by bit. She began by staying out very late at nights; next, she stayed gone for a whole week.

Finally, she left and never came back.

After she had been gone for several months, I realized how much I loved her and missed her. I guess the old adage is true, "Absence makes the heart grow fonder." The longer she was gone, the more frustrated I became. I decided that a good walk would help my frustration. I walked until I found myself back at the foot of Mount Tabor. Hastily I climbed to the top of the mountain and walked to the place where God had given me the outrageous assignment. I was hoping to find God there so I could remind Him that this was His doing and tell Him about the bitterness of my pain and disappointment.

Although I wanted to find God, I was astonished to find Him waiting for me. Immediately I said, "Did You not know what she was going to do? All along I considered the prospect of her backsliding a likely possibility; however I thought that I would make her happy enough that her focus would be toward the future and not to the past."

"Hosea, I know your pain," God said, "but first tell Me how you really feel about Gomer."

"You are aware of how she has treated me?"

"Yes, but that's not what I asked you. I want to know how you feel about her."

Then I said quite forcefully, "You are aware of how much I have been embarrassed and even reprimanded by the prophetic fraternity. At the last National Prophetic Convention of Israel, a proclamation was read concerning me, which in summary said, 'Gomer had stayed out and now moved out of Hosea's house.' It went further to state that I should be ostracized and held in contempt as a lover of illicit women. Because of this proclamation, my prophetic reputation and relationships with my fellow prophets have been permanently damaged."

"I know all of that," God said, "however, that's not what I asked you. What I want to know is how you feel about Gomer."

"Lord, if You only knew how difficult this is for me."

In a still soothing voice, God said to me, "I know Hosea."

"Are we alone; is anyone else around to hear our conversation?" I was not ready for anyone to hear my answer.

"No; no one is near," He said. "What is your confession?"

"As tough as it is for me to admit, I MUST CONFESS THAT I AM STILL VERY MUCH IN LOVE WITH GOMER."

As soon as I said this, God's voice suddenly rang out with heavenly delight. "That's good. If you can continue to love her despite what she has done to you, then you are ready to be My representative. Now, Hosea, you get off this mountain, run and tell Israel that the Lord their God and rightful husband does not wish to divorce them; instead He seeks restoration. Tell them that although Gomer has played the harlot, I have forgiven her of her adultery. Tell them that I still love her and that the unfaithfulness in your marriage, Hosea, was not about you and Gomer; it was really about God and Israel. I had divinely used the ugliness of your domestic difficulty to demonstrate the beauty of God's perfect love for those who are in the unlovely crowd."

You should have seen me getting off that mountain. I was running as fast as I could. I ran a while then rolled and rollicked down the mountain, my joy and gladness made the mountain seem like flatland. God had given me very good news, and as I made my way down the mountain, I heard God's voice call my name.

"Hosea, now one other thing."

"What now, Lord?"

"Hosea, before you speak to Israel, let Me speak directly to you. My concern about your marriage was not only about an unfaithful wife but also about an unforgiving husband. There are the Gomers of history; then there are the Hoseas of history. There are the prostitutes and the prophets, and they both have their weaknesses and failures."

Again I was offended that God not only seemed to overlook the fact that I was the victim, but now He was accusing me of having contributed to the failure of the marriage. He not only called my faithfulness into question but also my relationship with Him.

Did I really have an unlovely spirit; was I really an unforgiving prophet? Can something as simple as holding a grudge qualify as an ungodly sin? Of all people, God should understand my situation, as He knew how Israel played the harlot before Him for over seven hundred years.

God then said, "Just as My love embraces the unloveliness of an unfaithful wife, My love also embraces the unloveliness of an unforgiving prophet." He added, "It is ironic that those who have been forgiven are most often the most difficult ones from whom to receive forgiveness."

I admit it; this principle certainly displayed itself in my relationship with Gomer. I loved her and I hated her. I hated what she had become and I hated what it had caused her to do to me. Yet I genuinely and truly loved her. I loved the childlikeness beneath what was hidden behind her superficial exterior. What a strange paradox. I wanted revenge but at the same time entertained thoughts of her restoration.

In an effort to redeem our relationship, God reminded me of how much He had forgiven me and therefore how I should be willing to forgive Gomer for all the transgressions and sins she had committed against me.

Some of you, no doubt, also find it difficult to forgive. Like me, you have carried a torch for the person who wronged you for a long time. Although you have been forgiven by God, you find it extremely challenging to forgive others. Be reminded that God says those who claim to love Him yet hate their brothers or sisters do not have the love of God in them (according to 1 John 4:20).

I was surprised not only by God's theology but also by His sociology. I understood why wretchedness needed to be exposed to righteousness. I knew then that I needed my beliefs challenged in order to test their veracity and durability.

Through that unwanted relationship, He used the ugly truth of domestic difficulties in order to demonstrate God's love for the unlovely. I learned true piety will remain true. Even in the midst of the worst kind of depravity, it will remain humble, teachable, and loving.

The Lord said that when He tuned in on the frequency of my sermon, He noticed that my theology was missing a very important element. It was one-sided and out of context, He said. You see, my theology was a theology of justice without mercy. It was a theology of law without grace.

"Hosea, you've got to straighten up your understanding of Me," God explained.

"I AM NOT ALL JUSTICE; I AM ALSO MERCY. I AM NOT ALL WRATH; I'M ALSO A GOD OF SECOND CHANCES."

That is when I looked back over my life. It began to dawn on me that all of my life I had been taught an eye for an eye. All of my life I had been taught a tooth for a tooth. Whatever somebody does to you, you ought to do the exact same thing to that person. When my wife ruptured our relationship, when my wife allowed strange men to encroach upon my private domain, my training came out in me. I wanted an eye for an eye, and I wanted a tooth for a tooth. I had become ossified with my theology.

One day I was home taking care of the children; I went out in the field where I was trying to grow some food and noticed one of the men of Israel coming toward me. He called me by my name. "Prophet Hosea, I just left the marketplace. Prophet Hosea, you will never guess who I saw in the marketplace! I almost did not recognize her because the years of sin had taken their toll.

"It's your wife! The years of sin have stripped her of her beauty. She doesn't look like the same woman as when she was your wife, but I got a little closer because I recognized a certain peculiarity about her." He told me, "Your wife is downtown in the marketplace. She's being sold as a common slave."

Then I got up out of my field and made my way to the house. I went into my prayer room. I asked the Lord, "Lord, what do You want me to do?" He answered my question with a question.

"Hosea, how do you feel about her?"

I told him that I still loved her.

He then told me, “Hosea, you can’t quit now. You’ve got to do what you know is right and what will please and glorify Me in the end. So go and finish My story, Hosea.”

I reached up in my closet, and I put on my prophetic regalia. I wanted the people of Israel to know that I was wrapped up in the love of God. I wanted Israel to know that I was under divine unction.

I wrapped up in my prophetic regalia, and I began to walk the dusty streets of Judah. As I walked in the town, I could hear the crowd begin to whisper. You know how crowds are when families are in trouble. You know how friends talk when families are having trouble. You know how they try to keep you apart when families are having trouble. You know how they put in their own two cents when families are having trouble. I heard one gathering say, “There goes Hosea. He’s on his way to have the last laugh.” I heard one section of the crowd say, “There goes Hosea. He’s on his way to shake his vindictive finger in the face of his unfaithful wife.”

I made my way to the town's center, turned the corner by the grocery store, and then I heard a loud voice. An auctioneer, his phrases ringing loudly, declared, "We have a woman here. Her name is Gomer. We have a woman here. Her profession is prostitution. We have a woman here, but she has lost her beauty. We don't see any relatives.

IS THERE ANYBODY HERE WHO IS
WILLING TO PAY THE PRICE?"

I was standing in the back of the crowd. I was so afraid that he would not see my hand.

As I waved my hand, I said, "Mr. Auctioneer, my name is Hosea, and that wonderful woman is my wife. I know that she has mistreated me. I know that she is guilty of adultery. I know that she has lost her beauty, but I've come here today to pay the price. Whatever it is, I'll pay the price."

I took my wife by the hand and started on my way back home. However, on the way back home, the girl fell at my feet and said,

"HOSEA, I'LL BE YOUR SLAVE FOR THE REST OF MY LIFE."

I told her, "Get up, my darling. My children do not need a slave. They need a mother, and I need a wife."

And so I resumed our relationship and set about mending our broken marriage. I forgave her infidelity and adultery. I gave Gomer a second chance. I could not in good conscience abandon her, for God would not abandon our nation or me. I took back Gomer because I love her just as God loves me.

Well, that's my story. But you see, my story was just to prepare the way to tell you about another love story—the story of God's love. Shortly after Creation, man sinned. Then Justice stepped up and asked, "What shall be done with man's sin?" Then Justice said, "Let the wages of sin be death."

Jesus answered and said,

"The wages of sin is death;
but the free gift of God is eternal life."
(ROMANS 6:23)

God told Justice, "Go down to Mount Calvary and wait there for Jesus." Finally, one Friday, Jesus showed up with a cross on His shoulders. Justice, long awaiting the payment for sin, was finally and fully satisfied. For sin, Jesus was crucified and died. He was laid in a grave late Friday night. He stayed in the grave all day and all night Saturday. He paid the price to buy us back.

But early Sunday morning God raised Jesus from the dead. He now has all power in His hands. Oh sinner, He got up to save you! He got up to forgive you. He got up because He loves you.

You see, God specializes in second chances, and so no matter how far you may have drifted, no matter how dreadful your life, His love is available to you. Your life cannot outstretch the tender, limitless arms of God. God's love is deeper and wider than you can ever think or imagine. He is waiting for you to run into His arms and start trusting Him again.

If you come to Him, you'll find that
same peace.

If you come to Him, you can find that
same joy.

If you come to Him, you can find that
same forgiveness.

If you come to Him, you'll find that
same restoration.

If you come to Him, you'll find that
He'll save you right now!

SINCE 1894, Moody Publishers has been dedicated to equip and motivate people to advance the cause of Christ by publishing evangelical Christian literature and other media for all ages, around the world. Because we are a ministry of the Moody Bible Institute of Chicago, a portion of the proceeds from the sale of this book go to train the next generation of Christian leaders.

If we may serve you in any way in your spiritual journey toward understanding Christ and the Christian life, please contact us at www.moodypublishers.com.

"All Scripture is God-breathed and is useful for teaching, rebuking, correcting and training in righteousness, so that the man of God may be thoroughly equipped for every good work."

—2 Timothy 3:16, 17

THE NAME YOU CAN TRUST®